P9-CQY-469

SCHOLASTIC'S
A+ JUNIOR GUIDE
TO STUDYING

LOUISE COLLIGAN

Lisa
Altobelli

SCHOLASTIC INC.
New York Toronto London Auckland Sydney

Book design by Ira Hechtlinger

ISBN 0-590-40590-X

12 11 10 9 8 7 6

1 2/9

Printed in the U.S.A.

40

First Scholastic printing, August 1987

*To the students
of the Irvington, New York, Middle School*

Table of Contents

1
How To Organize Yourself
on the Home Front

Did your first weeks in middle school go something like this?

• You couldn't find half your classes on the first try?

• Your locker combination wouldn't unlock at the worst possible times?

• You had a hard time figuring out your schedule for all those classes? Or, worse, you lost your schedule completely?

• Your notebook, the one you bought right before school started, vanished the first week or was the wrong kind?

• The eighth graders hassled you and your friends every chance they got?

In short, was middle school a pretty confusing place to go to five days a week?

If these things happened to you, please know

that you are not alone. Over and over the little things make school hard for some students. You do your homework but forget it on the bus. You show up a little late for class and miss out on important announcements. You listen attentively in class but forget your notebook at home. You read the wrong chapter or memorize the wrong spelling list. Pretty soon these small mistakes add up. You do nearly as much work as A students but wind up with lower grades. You just miss the mark, not out of laziness or lack of brain cells, but because you aren't sure how to organize your work.

Well, guess what? *Everybody*, from the class brain to the class clown, has some problems managing school in the middle grades. Different classes, different teachers, lots more homework and tests, older kids — many of these things overwhelm students.

To find out what problems were bugging students in school, a large group was asked this question: *"What was the hardest thing you remember about starting middle school?"*

Here are some of the answers:
- *". . . knowing where the classes were."*
- *". . . getting used to older kids."*
- *". . . being teased by eighth graders."*

2

- *". . . switching from class to class."*
- *". . . having too many teachers."*
- *". . . getting my locker opened."* (Nearly every student mentioned this!)
- *". . . having too many subjects."*
- *". . . learning my schedule."*
- *". . . figuring out what class came next."*
- *". . . doing homework in all different subjects."*
- *". . . keeping my locker neat."* (There are those lockers again!)

The students who made these comments had somehow managed to survive at least one year of middle school. So the next question asked them was: *"Now that you have been in middle school for a while, what advice would you give to a new student who is just starting the middle grades?"*

Here are some of the answers:
- *"Don't fall asleep in class!"*
- *"Pay attention."*
- *"Reread everything."*
- *"Save all your notes and the teachers' dittos."*
- *"Don't be nervous; it'll get better."*
- *"Be on time."*
- *"Don't do your homework or study for a test at the last minute."*

- *"Don't be obnoxious."*
- *"Don't worry about it; just do it."*
- *"Take notes."*
- *"Don't aggravate older kids."*
- *"Don't worry if you don't make friends the first day."*
- *"You'll get used to it."*
- *"Do your work all the time; don't let it pile up."*
- *"Don't worry about other kids. Just be yourself, and if they're really going to be your friends, they'll accept you that way."*
- *"Don't be afraid to ask your teacher things."*
- *"Keep everything in one notebook."*
- *"Don't show off."*
- *"Stay home!"*
- *"Be organized."*
- *"It gets easier."*

Take another look at the last three comments. This book is written for those of you who have gotten so frustrated by school that you sometimes wish you could stay home. "Be organized" is the best piece of advice on this list, and this book is going to show you *exactly* how to do it. No matter what your IQ is; no matter what you look like, what you wear, or what you eat for breakfast, getting organized is something you will be able to do if you follow some of the advice in this book.

Here's a quiz to help you know how to be organized. Check off YES or NO next to each item.

Quiz Yourself on Being Organized

YES	NO	
☑	☑	I have a special study area at home with supplies, dictionary, bulletin board, calendar, etc.
☑	☐	I have a calendar at home to keep track of important dates.
☑	☑	I write down all my important due dates and appointments where I'll notice them.
☑	☐	I have my school schedule written in a handy place.
☑	☐	I have the phone number of someone in each of my classes.
☑	☑	I have an alarm clock to wake me up in the morning.
☑	☐	I have a book bag, backpack, or tote bag for school.
☑	☐	I have an assignment pad or a date book I keep handy.
☑	☑	I write down all my assignments.

YES	NO	
☑	☐	I have a notebook divided by subjects.
☑	☐	I usually have my notebook when I need it.
☑	☐	I pick out what I'm going to wear the night before.
☑	☐	I am usually on time for the bus or for school.

Here's what to do now. Circle all your NO answers. Then, in the following spaces, write them down in the order in which you want to change each NO to a YES. Here's a tip to help you get started. Write down the *easiest* item first so that you can get going on it the fastest. Save the hardest steps for last.

I want to get a
notebook and an
ogradser Diary and
I cant every thing.
Oginised

_____

_____

_____

_____

_____

_____

_____

Decide today to work on each habit, *one by one*. If one step is too hard, try a different one. Don't try to change yourself overnight by doing everything on this list all at once. That's like trying to learn to play a musical instrument in a week! Take your time with each step. As you complete each goal, cross it out. If some goals seem too hard for now, write them down on the Goal Sheet on pages 78–79. Then, a few months from now, try working on those goals again. You'll be amazed at what a few months can do.

Making Organizing Easy

Think of all the space you have found for things that matter to you. Perhaps you've got a closet and dresser for your clothes. Maybe a hallway or closet for sports equipment. A couple of shelves for collections of rocks, stuffed animals, trophies, bottlecaps, trading cards, insects, or camp ribbons. How about giving some space to your school stuff?

Here's what you need:

1. *A bulletin board, wall space, or the back of a door.* This is where you are going to put everything that matters to you — the autographed picture of your favorite music group, your precious tickets to the upcoming rock show, and a wall calendar with big white spaces.

2. *Wall calendar.* This is the place to keep track of your busy life from now on. Circle the super-important dates in BIG RED LETTERS!!!!! WRITE DOWN EVERYTHING AS IT COMES UP EACH AND EVERY TIME — from after-school dates to test deadlines; from orthodontist appointments to band practice. You'll be amazed at how easily you will remember important dates and jobs once you take that extra step of putting them on your calendar.

3. *Extra class schedule.* Put this on your bulletin board, too, so that you can check your next day's schedule to find out if you have a free period before math or not.

4. *The phone number of one student in each class.* When you miss a class or get stuck on homework, it's great to have someone you can call on for help.

5. *A flat surface to write on.* This can be a desk, a

piece of shelving resting on bricks, a tray to put over your knees (if you do your best writing in bed or sitting on the floor).

6. *Tape, scissors, magic markers, pens, pencils, thumbtacks or pushpins, clips, and extra notebook paper.* Store all this in a spare drawer, bookshelf, or box, so you can find everything fast without searching all over the house.

7. *A three-ring notebook with dividers for each subject.* This is the kind to have unless your teachers require something different. A three-ring notebook is a great organizer. Now you'll have a place to put all those purple handout sheets that have been floating around in your locker and backpack. Those ditto sheets contain most of the questions — *and answers* — that will be on nearly every test you take. Any teacher who goes through all the trouble of getting purple ink all over her fingers and shirt cuffs thinks the information she is copying is pretty important. So get those stray sheets into your notebook right away.

Inside the cover of this notebook tape a copy of your schedule.

8. *A steno-style assignment pad.* This is where you first write down each of your daily homework assignments. Most students clip this to the inside cover of their three-ring notebooks.

9. *A book bag or backpack to carry all your important stuff to school.* Where are you going to put your packs of gum, wallet, camouflage pencils, and favorite novel if you don't have something to tote them around in? A book bag or backpack is also handy for transporting your three-ring notebook, textbooks, and school supplies. Don't leave home without it!

10. *An alarm clock.* This is an alternative to the sound of nagging voices at seven A.M.

11. *Optional but great to have:* a dictionary, thesaurus, and library card; a wristwatch; a tape recorder to help you memorize spelling and vocabulary lists, multiplication tables, and math rules.

Now that you're all equipped for home and school, what else do you need to make your job as a student even easier? How about more time?

Ten Terrific Time-Savers

1. Lay out your next day's clothes, book bag, keys, money, and homework each school night. Check your assignment pad and calendar to make sure you have everything you will need for the next day. Know the night before what you have to do the next day.

2. Make your next day's lunch the night before, if you bring your own lunch to school. Do it right after dinner, and you'll get first crack at the best leftovers.

3. Shower or wash your hair at night instead of in the morning.

4. Have a set bedtime for school nights. Your parents may have one for you — maybe too early. You might be able to negotiate a later hour if you can prove to them that you can get out of bed on your own and on time. If you can't, then stick to the earlier bedtime, or start going to bed five minutes earlier every night until you can get yourself up without feeling super-tired for more than the first five minutes. (Let's face it. The first five minutes up are the worst. If you're still really tired after that, you are going to bed too late.)

5. If morning fights over the bathroom are daily events at your house, negotiate with members of your family to use the bathroom at a set time *for* a set time. Haircombing and dressing can all be done in your room.

6. Never, ever fight in the morning. It takes up too much time and ruins your day. You can always fight later, but you can't catch the school bus later.

7. Do as much homework as you can in school

during free periods, lunchtime, or on the bus. However, if school hours are the only time to see your friends, save your homework for home.

8. Each week, take the TV listing and circle everything you plan to watch that week. Don't watch anything you haven't circled. Say there's a terrific movie scheduled one night in the week. That day, plan to do your homework at school or in the afternoon so that you'll be completely free to watch the movie without feeling guilty about undone homework.

9. Do two things at once. While you're watching TV or listening to music, you can: exercise, sew on missing buttons, iron a shirt, clean out your notebook, sort out a bureau drawer, work on your scrapbook or photo album, write a thank-you note, organize your records, do a crossword or jigsaw puzzle, clean out your book bag. Reminder: Homework is a one-at-a-time job, not to be done in front of television or to the sound of rock 'n' roll. Isn't it a lot more fun to enjoy your favorite programs without having a page of fractions in front of you? Get your homework out of the way first, then treat yourself to guilt-free television.

10. Try to work out regular calling times with your friends so that you can have good, long

conversations without worrying about that English or social studies assignment. Talking to a friend is a good way to reward yourself for finishing all your homework.

Now that you have gotten your home life in shape, you are ready to take on school.

2
How To Organize Yourself at School

It's eight-twenty-nine A.M. You made it out of your house in record time. The book bag under the bus seat contains your completed homework, books, pencils, the lunch you made last night, and your flute. (You remembered your flute because you wrote down "band practice" on your calendar.) You are so organized for school, you can hardly believe it. You lean back in your seat, confident that Mr. Whizwell, your science teacher, won't catch you off guard without your notebook again.

And for once, you had that vocabulary ditto right where you could find it. Mrs. Wordley, your English teacher, can go right ahead and ask you what *ornery* means. You even remembered to bring in the $3 you need to go on the planetarium trip. According to this book, you should be all set for the day.

So why do you wish today were Saturday? Probably because you're wondering just how having a neat notebook with little colored dividers is going to get you better grades. Or how your teacher's supposed to know you've made three copies of your schedule. You may be wondering how being organized at home is going to have any effect on this bell-ringing, crowded, noisy, and demanding place called school.

Well, having a copy of your schedule everywhere you go, owning a three-ring notebook, saving all your dittos and putting them into that notebook, *writing down absolutely everything* — these habits are going to pay off.

Now it's time to consider what in-school habits you can work on to make your school day a lot easier. On page 16 is another quiz to help you figure out what good habits you already have so that you can work on the habits you *ought* to have. Check off YES or NO next to each item below.

Quiz Yourself on Being Organized at School

YES	NO	**Lockers:**
☑	☐	I usually arrive at school with everything I need that day.
☐	☑	I finally figured out my locker combination.
☑	☐	I have my class schedule taped inside my locker.
☑	☐	I keep a few emergency school supplies in my locker.
☑	☐	I can usually find what I'm looking for in my locker in less than a minute.
☑	☐	I am usually on time for my classes.
☑	☐	I usually have what I need for each class.

		Listening and Note-Taking:
☑	☐	I am a good listener in class.
☑	☐	I write down what the teacher tells the class to write down.
☑	☐	I usually raise my hand when I know the answers.
☑	☐	I ask the teacher or another student if I am confused about something.

16

YES	NO	**Listening and Note-Taking:**
	☑	I always write down the homework in my assignment pad.
		General Class Behavior:
☑	☐	I rarely have to be reminded to keep quiet in class.
☑	☐	I get along with my teachers.
☑	☐	I am pretty good at managing all my different classes.

How many YES answers do you have? Whatever the number, keep up the good work. Now circle your NO answers and write them down here. One by one, changing the NO to YES will be the goal to set for yourself in the next few weeks.

_____

_____

_____

_____

_____

_____

_____

_____

_____

Work on the easiest goals first just to give yourself a boost. If you can't seem to accomplish one of the steps on your list, forget it for now. Move on to something easier. When you reach each goal, cross it out. If you have any left over that are too hard to do now, list them on pages 78–79.

Making Organizing Easy

1. Lockers

A. *Stuck lock.* Lockers seem to be an awful daily problem for many kids. You are not alone if you find yourself frantically whirling your combination in between classes, and the thing still doesn't open. Here's a solution. During your free time, try to get your locker open several times in a row. Keep practicing until you can almost do it blindfolded. Make sure you have a written copy of the combination numbers in your book bag, notebook, or at home. Another solution to locker madness is to carry around what you need for the day. That way you don't have to deal with your locker in between classes when you are rushed.

B. *Class schedule.* Keep a copy inside your locker. If you succeed in getting your locker open between classes, you may find yourself looking at a stack of books and not knowing where you're supposed to go next. That's what your schedule is there for.

C. *Supplies.* Keep a few extra supplies in your locker for those occasional days when you forget your notebook or book bag. That way you won't have to show up empty-handed for class.

If your classes are miles apart, don't stop at your locker between classes. Instead, carry a morning or afternoon's worth of what you need.

D. *Locker neatness.* Your locker doesn't have to be spotless. But it should be neat enough for you to find what you need in those critical few minutes between classes. If it takes you more than a few seconds to find your stuff in a hurry, get rid of the banana peels. Gather up all your old tests and put them in a folder at home. (You can use them to study for final exams.) Get those free-floating teacher dittos into your notebook. If you think of it, right before each vacation starts, clear out those gum wrappers, crazy notes from your friends, and anything that looks moldy or half alive. That way you'll come back to a clean locker after vacation.

2. Being on Time

Usually students forget how short a three-minute break is. Three minutes — or five — is probably enough time to get to class directly, but it's nowhere near enough time to catch up on the latest gossip with your friends. Nothing is more aggravating to teachers than making an announcement and having two or three kids drift in late (or rush in all out of breath). *Class lateness, missing notebooks, and not writing things down are three of the surest ways to lower your grades.* If you beat these bad habits, you can probably raise yourself one whole grade — all without having to study one extra minute! Use the extra time you save to have fun!

3. Being Equipped

Going to school is a job. Carpenters have saws and hammers; mechanics have wrenches; and teachers have briefcases and red markers. Students like you need special equipment, too: the class textbook, your three-ring notebook, an assignment pad, writing materials, and the current completed homework assignment. These are your tools, and if you show up in class empty-handed, you might as well be wearing a sign that says I DON'T CARE! You wouldn't be reading these words right now if you didn't care. So get it together — the class book, notebook, assignment pad, pens and pencils. Stash it all in a book bag and show up for your job properly equipped.

4. Listening Skills

Does your mind go blank five minutes after class? Do your classes seem to be all talk with no point? When you study for tests, is it hard to remember what your teacher said was important? You don't need a hearing test, but you might find the following tips on listening skills helpful. Here is how to begin listening to what is going on in class:

A. *Do all your written homework and reading.* The work will give you an idea of what the teacher thinks is important and what he or she will probably talk about in class.

B. *Be on time.* Most teachers start each class by announcing what they are going to talk about the rest of the period. If you stroll in late, you will have to fill in the missing pieces.

C. *Open your notebook when you sit down.* Write down any questions you have as the teacher is talking. Then ask the questions before class is over.

D. *Make eye contact with your teacher.* You'll find it easier to concentrate and follow what's being said if you watch your teacher as she or he speaks. This will also keep you from daydreaming or noticing that your best friend is clowning around. If you are allowed to choose your own seat, sit near the front. It's easier to hear what's going on close up. And you won't be as distracted by other kids sitting behind you.

E. *Stay awake.* Get yourself involved in class. Ask questions. Answer questions. Take notes.

F. *If you wear glasses, wear them!* Seeing clearly will help you listen better.

G. *On a bad day, talk to another student after class.* You are going to have tired, daydreamy days once in a while. When that happens, borrow another student's notes or ask someone about the class.

5. Taking Notes

In middle school, you usually don't have to write down too many class notes. But when you do, here is what to write down:

A. *Write down the date on each set of notes and ditto sheets.*

B. *Save all handout sheets in your notebook.* Most middle school teachers take notes for you on handout sheets. If your teacher talks about the handout sheet in class, write down anything that sounds important right on the sheet. Or underline it. File each handout sheet in the proper section of your notebook right away. Before you begin your homework, look over the ditto sheet or your notes from that day. If you take five minutes to do this, your homework will be easier. And you will also save a lot of studying at test time.

C. *Write it down*. If your teacher says, "Write it down," write it down!

D. *Copy this*. If your teacher writes something on the board or says, "Copy this," copy it.

E. *Set apart important information*. Put stars, rainbows, or lightning bolts around information your teacher says is going to be on a test.

F. *Borrow*. Borrow another student's notes or handouts if you miss a class or were daydreaming. Or see your teacher about any missing notes or assignments when you return to planet Earth.

G. *Write down the homework assignment and due date in your assignment book.*

6. Dealing with Friends, Enemies, Difficult Teachers, and Hard Classes

A. *Friends and enemies*. Do you know these people? *The pilot* is the guy who takes the teacher's dittos and turns them into sleek aircraft. *The whisperer* carries on forty-minute conversations without getting distracted by the sound of a teacher's voice. *The note passer* passes on yesterday's gossip on little slips of paper. *The noisemaker* has perfected all the sounds of the animal kingdom and turns the class into a zoo. *The comedian* can't resist just one more joke. Do some of these characters sound a little too familiar? That may be why you have a hard time paying attention in class. Kids who clown around are often the very students having trouble in school. That's why they act up. Try not to be a sidekick in class; you can always talk to your friends later.

B. *Difficult teachers.* Sooner or later, every student gets a teacher who is hard to get along with. What do you do about that?

Here are some ways to cope:

• Make sure you are always *extra-prepared* for this teacher's class. This alone will cut down on the number of conflicts. A teacher can't complain that you haven't done your homework if you have. A teacher can't tell you you're sloppy if your work is neat. A teacher can't hassle you about your behavior if you show up on time, prepared, and sit there quietly taking notes.

• If a teacher seems to pick on you and your usual reaction is to yell back, try counting to ten instead.

• Talk to your homeroom teacher or one of your parents. They may have some advice. Or they may make you feel better by agreeing with you.

C. *Hard classes.* Suppose one reason you hate a certain class is because it's hard, and you don't understand the work. That's enough to make you crawl under the covers on a Monday morning, isn't it?

Here are some ways to make a hard class easier:

• Spend twice as much study time on a hard class as on an easy one.

• Do the hardest homework first, when you are most alert.

• Learn to ask questions or ask the teacher to repeat information in a hard class. See the teacher after class if you still need help. When a teacher knows you are really trying, you may get extra help and a little more sympathy.

• Find a friend in class who is good in the subject. See if he or she can explain it to you more easily.

• Write down the homework assignments, word for word.

• Be especially careful about taking class notes.

• Go to the school library and ask the librarian if there's an easier book on the subject for a lower grade.

• Have someone look over your homework — an older brother or sister, a parent, or a student who is good in the subject.

• Always read over your corrected homework, tests, and papers in a hard class. You should do this for all your subjects, but it's even more important in a difficult one. Save all your work so you can see what it is that keeps tripping you up.

• If your teacher or parents suggest getting a tutor, get one. Yes, it's a pain, but it will pay off. Otherwise, this subject is always going to be hard for you. You probably have at least ten more years of school left. Do you want ten more years of hating math? Fix the problem now while you can.

Hang in there! You can do it!

3
How To Take the Work
Out of Homework

"If only we didn't have homework."
"Oh, no, I forgot my homework again!"
"I did my homework, but it's a mess."
"I can't watch TV till I do my homework."
"I can't go out till I do my homework."
"My life would be perfect if only I didn't have homework."

Sound familiar? If there's one thing nearly every student complains about, it's homework. Just a few years ago, you probably got on the school bus with nothing more in your backpack than some Kleenex, an extra sweater, and a small notebook. Now you go home like a pack mule, sinking under the weight of textbooks, notebooks, and papers. What is causing this daily problem with gravity? HOMEWORK! Ten out of ten middle school kids would probably rather have no homework than have hot fudge sundaes at lunch every day.

Homework follows you right out of the school building like a storm cloud. You go home, and right there in the refrigerator is the homework cloud. Should you do your homework first or make yourself a snack? You just want to flop on the couch, flick on the TV for a few minutes, and let your mind go blank. But no, there's homework following you around again. The doorbell rings. It's your friend next door, suggesting a quick bike ride to the soccer field. You say yes, but that homework cloud hanging over everything takes away the fun of making plans.

If only you didn't have homework! But unfortunately you do. Let's face it. The solution is to *do the homework as painlessly as possible*. And that's what this chapter is all about.

First you have to figure out what it is about homework that's bothering you. Maybe what's ruining your life in the homework department isn't the actual work but finding the time to do it. Or maybe you keep leaving the homework sheets in school. Let's take a look at what works and doesn't work for you when it comes to homework. Check off YES or NO to the following statements.

Quiz Yourself on Homework

YES	NO	In Class:
☑	☑	I write down all my assignments and the due dates.
☑	☑	I ask the teacher questions about parts of the homework I'm not sure about.
☑	☐	Before I leave class, I know what books and papers I'll need to do the assignment.
☑	☐	I leave school with everything I need to do all my homework.

YES	NO	At Home:
☐	☑	I have figured out the best time of day to schedule my homework.
☑	☑	I write down future projects and tests on my calendar in big letters. I check my calendar every day to see if anything important is coming up soon.
☑	☐	I rarely postpone doing my homework.
☑	☐	I work on the hardest homework first.

YES	NO	At Home:
☑	☐	I do a little bit every day on big projects or tests that are coming up.
☑	☐	I write down questions about parts of the homework I don't understand.
☐	☑	I have a friend or someone in my family I can ask about the homework I don't understand.
☑	☐	I reread each assignment when I finish it. I check that it is neat and complete, and has the right punctuation and spelling.
☑	☐	I check my assignment pad when I finish my homework to check if I have done it all.
☑	☐	I put my homework and books in my book bag.
☐	☑	I put my book bag by the door or in a place where I can grab it quickly in the morning.

Follow-up:

☐	☑	I usually have my homework on hand when the teacher collects it.

YES	NO	Follow-up:
☑	☑	My homework is usually marked good or satisfactory.
☑	☐	I save all my homework to study from at test time.

Do you have some YES answers? Good! Now circle the NO answers and copy them below. Write them down in the order that will be easiest for you to work on. If there are goals you would like to work toward later on, write them on the Goal Sheet on pages 78–79.

_____

_____

_____

_____

_____

_____

_____

_____

_____

_____

_____

_____

_____

_____

_____

_____

_____

Managing Your Homework

Here are suggestions for accomplishing each goal on the list. Remember, work on just one at a time. If something is too hard to do right now, try a different step. You can always go back to any of these steps later. Just doing one thing on this list is better than trying too many at once and getting discouraged.

1. *Write it down.* Copy down the homework, due dates, and the materials you'll need to do the homework.

2. *Ask the teacher to explain what you don't understand about the homework.* Sometimes kids have problems with homework because they don't know quite what they are supposed to do. If you are uncertain about the homework, ask your teacher to explain the directions or examples again. Or ask a classmate right after class.

3. *Bring home all the materials for each day's homework.* Recheck your assignment pad before you go home. Check your book bag to make sure everything you will need is in there.

4. *Set aside a block of time every day just for homework. When* you do your homework isn't as important as making time for it. Some days you can wrap it up in a free period. Other times you might want to see friends during your free period, so you'll do your homework at home. If you know a favorite TV show is on that night, do your homework as soon as you get home. Some kids like to (or are required to) do their homework at a specified time every day. Figure out what time works best for *you.*

5. *Check your calendar every day for long-term assignments.* A long-term, two-week deadline shrinks fast. Get in the habit of looking at your big calendar every day to see what's coming up soon.

6. *Work on the hardest homework first.* Why? You need the most brainpower for harder jobs than easier ones. Usually people have the most energy and concentration at the beginning of a task. However, there are some students who need to do easier work first just to get their wheels going. Try both ways to see which is better for you.

7. *Mark sections or write down questions next to*

33

homework you don't understand. A lot of students turn in poor homework because they get stuck on a problem or are confused about the directions. Sometimes they are too afraid to tell the teacher about the problems they had.

Here's what to do when you get stuck on homework:

• Complete all the homework that you can. Then reread your assignment pad, class notes, or the part of your textbook that applies to your homework. Maybe you will find the answer in one of those places.

• Do what you can on the problem homework first. Then work on your easier homework. Later on, go back to what you didn't understand. A problem might be easier to solve the second time around.

• If you still can't complete all the homework, call a friend in class for help. See if your school, library, or local college has a homework hotline. Give it a call. Or, as a last resort, ask a family member for advice.

• If you are still stuck, write a note to your teacher, asking for help on the parts you couldn't do. Attach the note to your homework. Go to class a few minutes early. Show your teacher the homework you *did* do and ask for help on the rest. See if you can get a one-night extension to complete the assignment. Or if you have a free period later, see if you can bring in the assignment at the end of the day. These are all steps to try when you have homework problems. Just make sure you talk to your teacher *before* you turn in an incomplete assignment.

8. *Reread each assignment as you finish it.* Take this very short extra step to check that there are no examples or words missing. See if you have all the right punctuation and spelling. Neatness counts for a lot. Recopy any sloppy work. Teachers don't give points for spots of spaghetti on your homework!

9. *Recheck your assignment pad when you finish your homework.* Make sure you have done *all* your homework in every subject. This advice holds true for homework, writing assignments, and tests. *Always reread directions to make sure you did what you were supposed to do.*

10. *Gather your homework in your book bag. Put the bag where you'll see it the next day.* Every student has had at least one awful day of getting on the bus empty-handed. What an awful feeling, especially if you've done the homework. Since mornings are such a rush, put your book bag right by the door every night.

11. *Bring your homework to class.* Easier said than done sometimes, when your locker is miles away. It's worth repeating that you should work out a regular system for gathering all your materials from your locker at certain times of day.

12. *If you get poor marks on homework, find out why.* It's painful to get back homework with negative comments. The way to prevent that next time around is to find out why. See your teacher about what you did wrong. Or ask a family member to help you figure out what the problem is.

13. *Save your homework.* You may not ever want to see those awful pages and pages of fractions. But your homework papers are some of the best study tools for future quizzes and exams. At test time, read over your old homework. See where you made mistakes. Here's an inside tip. Keep in mind that teachers often take test questions right from the previous homework. So store your homework in your notebook, or in a special folder at home, so you'll have it on hand at test time.

How To Read so You Will Remember What You've Read

Probably a lot of your homework is reading. Your teacher gives you so many pages to read. You read them. But many students have a hard time remembering what they have read the next day or at test time. If you just read through everything quickly when it's assigned, you are going to have to read it all over again when you get ready for a test. Want an easier way? Here are some pointers:

Reading Textbooks

To qualify as a textbook, a book has to weigh at least two pounds and cause bulges in your book bag! They make for heavy carrying and heavy reading. Here is how to lighten the textbook reading load:

1. *When you first get a textbook, read the Table of Contents.* That's the listing in front of the book that tells you where certain chapters are. The Table of Contents tells you — in a shortcut way — what the whole book is about. If you haven't done this yet with the textbooks you have now, read the Table of Contents before your next reading assignment. Why? Because this tells you what has been covered already and what's coming up. This will help you fit new information into a special slot.

2. *Read all the heavy black titles in a reading assignment twice.* Do this once before you start the main reading and once after you have read the material. These headings are clues about what you will be reading or have just read.

3. *Read any questions listed at the end of the chapter before you read.* This might sound like a backward way of doing things, but here's the reason: Those questions alert you to important information and ideas in the reading.

4. *Read through most of your reading assignments just once.*

But reread the following *twice:*

• Words in heavy black type — titles, headings.

• First and last sentences of each section under the heavy black type.

• Charts and pictures. If the information in these weren't important, the company that printed the book wouldn't hire an artist or photographer to illustrate it.

5. *Look up words you don't understand in your dictionary.* Keep a student dictionary by your side whenever you read.

6. *Write down page numbers and sections you don't understand.* If you are confused by some information, make a note of it to ask your teacher the next day.

Reading Stories and Novels

These are usually the easiest and most fun to read. Read through fiction (made-up stories, plays, novels) once. If you don't understand what you have read, skim the material fast, then once more, slowly. Use your dictionary to look up words you don't know.

When you finish a reading assignment on this kind of book, ask yourself these two questions:

1. Who were the main characters (the most important people in this part of the book)?

2. What were the three most important things that happened in what I just read?

You don't have to answer these questions to anyone but yourself. And you can do it in your head. This only takes about a minute or two but will go a long way in helping you remember the book. Try it!

4
How To Become
a Better Test Taker

Know what is right up there with homework as something kids dread? You guessed it — tests! There you are sailing along in school. You have gotten pretty organized at home and in class. Your locker could pass an Army inspection. Your notebook is as neat as a filing cabinet. Your homework assignments have been coming back with smiley faces on them.

Then, *bam!* Your teacher announces the first big test of the semester. Suddenly you're right back down in the pits again. You can't remember one single thing you learned all term. Butterflies crash around in your stomach. And until that test is over with, you are convinced you will not have a single moment of fun.

You don't even know where to begin getting ready for the test. Are you supposed to read your whole textbook all over again? Memorize every word you ever wrote down in class? Give up all TV and fun until it's over?

Thoughts of natural disasters run through your mind. Maybe you'll get seventy inches of snow the night before the test. Or you'll get another round of chicken pox and have to miss the test. Or your teacher will have her baby right on that day and forget to tell the substitute about the big test. Maybe some outside event will save you from having to take this awful test.

Wouldn't that be great? Sure it would, but it would also be pretty unlikely. Chicken pox only comes around once; teachers give tests before, during, and after blizzards. And you can't always count on a baby arriving at your convenience.

So what's the answer? *You* are. You can't control nature, but you can take some steps to improve your test scores.

Students have a lot to say about test taking. These middle school students, like you, sometimes hate school, sometimes enjoy it, and sometimes just get through. They were asked: *"What advice would you give new middle school students about taking tests?"*

This is what they said about their own experiences:
- *"Ask the teacher what is going to be on the test."*
- *"Study ahead of time."*
- *"Don't cram."*
- *"Study with a friend and quiz each other ahead of time."*
- *"Start studying early. Do a little bit at a time."*
- *"Don't throw out any papers the teacher gave you."*
- *"Do your work all the time. Don't let it pile up."*
- *"Memorize the important stuff."*
- *"Don't be nervous!"*

So how do you go about not being nervous? By knowing what good habits you already have; then thinking of new ones you could use. Here's a quiz to sort out what needs fixing from what doesn't, when it comes to taking a big test. Check off YES or NO to the statements below. Keep in mind that you don't need to do all the steps when you're taking a short test.

Quiz Yourself on Test Taking

YES	NO	
		In-Class Preparation:
☐	☑	I always write down test dates in my assignment pad.
☑	☐	Before I leave the class I know what is going to be covered on the test.
		Home Preparation:
☐	☑	I copy the test date in HUGE LET-TERS on my calendar.
☑	☐	I make up a plan to study for the test a few minutes every night, then longer the night before.
☑	☐	I try not to make any plans the night before a test.
		My study plan includes:
☑	☐	• catching up on any work I missed.
☐	☑	• rereading my class notes and handout sheets.
☑	☐	• rereading my old tests and homework papers.
☐	☑	• skimming my textbook.
☑	☐	• memorizing.
☑	☐	• quizzing myself the night before.

YES	NO	Taking the Test:
☑	☐	I arrive in class with everything my teacher said to bring for the test.
☑	☐	I listen carefully to the teacher's directions. I know how long I have, how many questions have to be answered, and whether to use pen or pencil.
☑	☐	I write down my name and the date the very first thing.
☑	☐	I read the directions carefully.
☑	☐	I look over the whole test to see what I have to do.
☐	☑	I figure out how much time I have to spend on each question.
☑	☐	I read each question carefully before I answer it.
☑	☐	I work on all the easiest problems first to give myself as many points as possible. (However, if some sections are worth the most, I work on the easiest examples of those sections first.)
☑	☐	I go back and answer any questions I skipped.
☑	☐	I double-check my answers.

YES	NO	Taking the Test:
☑	☐	I listen carefully when the teacher goes over my corrected test. Or I go over it myself to learn from my mistakes.
☑	☐	I save all my old tests as study sheets for final exams.

Do you already do some of the things on this list before a big test? Great! Now all you have to do is add a few more good habits to your list. Circle all your NO statements and write them below.

_____

_____

_____

_____

_____

_____

_____

_____

_____

_____

_____

Getting in Shape for Tests

Pretest Shape-up

1. *Write down the test date.* This is your first step in getting ready for a test. Once you know the date, figure out how many days you have to prepare for it.

2. *Find out what is going to be covered on the test.* If a math test is only going to include long division, spend all your study time on that, not on fractions or multiplication.

3. *Listen for clues in class.* Teachers want you to do as well on tests as you can. They want you to remember important information and ideas. Often in the days before a big test, a teacher will go over what the class has been studying. This is the time to get your notes up-to-date or underline important parts of the notes you already have. If your science teacher keeps repeating the word *camouflage*, that probably means you are going to be tested on it.

At-Home Shape-up

1. *Copy your test date on a big calendar.*

2. *What to do a few days before the test.* Set aside a few minutes a night to catch up on missing work and go over old homework, dittos, or tests. If there

are parts of the work you don't understand, get help. Start memorizing what your teacher said to memorize.

3. *Memorizing tips:*

• Make sure you understand what you are supposed to memorize.

• Do a little bit of memorizing each day.

• Do your memorizing steps at the beginning of each study period, when your mind is most alert.

• Write down, reread, or say out loud what you are trying to memorize, until you can recite the information without looking at it.

• If you have a tape recorder, use it to study spelling and vocabulary lists or multiplication and division tables. Say the information into your tape recorder and keep playing it back.

4. *What to do the night before the test.* Skim your textbook and reread anything that looks important in the book or in your notebook. If you have time, think up some questions you think your teacher might ask, and see if you can answer them in your head. Sometimes teachers ask questions that are similar to the ones listed at the end of chapters in your textbook. You might look those over to help yourself get ready. If you had material to memorize,

have someone in your family give you a quick oral quiz the night before. Or quiz yourself to see if you know the information inside out.

5. *Line up everything you will need for the test.* Go to bed early so you will be rested the next day. Have a good breakfast the day of the test.

Test-Time Shape-up

If you have done most of these steps, you should walk in on test day totally confident that you are going to do well. Here's what to do next:

1. *Arrive on time and have what you need.* Give yourself a little extra time on test day to get to class early. Bring a couple of pens, pencils, and an eraser to class. If you feel nervous in spite of everything, try this. Take a deep breath and let it out slowly. Or doodle on a scrap of paper.

2. *Listen carefully to your teacher.* Make sure you know how long you have for the test and what exactly you are supposed to do. Should you use pen or pencil? Is scrap paper allowed for figuring? Can you use a dictionary? If you are not sure about the spoken directions, ask your teacher to repeat them.

3. *Write your name and date on the paper first thing.*

4. *Read any written directions slowly.* Underline parts of the directions that seem important. Before

you write anything, you should know how much time you have; how many questions you are supposed to answer; what points each section is worth so that you can spend the most time on the most valuable questions.

5. *Give yourself a few minutes at the beginning to skim over the whole test.* This will give you an idea of what the whole test is about.

6. *Go down the sheet and do the easiest questions first* (if all questions are worth the same. If some are worth more than others, do the easiest of those first). Then go back to the beginning and tackle the next-easiest questions.

7. *Reread harder questions.* Underline important words to help yourself understand the question better. *Don't get stuck on a question.* Move on to questions you *can* answer, until you have gotten through all of those. Your goal is to gain as many points as possible.

8. *Guess answers.* If you are going to get the same number of points taken off for an incomplete answer, then you might as well take a good guess at it. Maybe you'll get some credit for part of your answer.

9. *When you are sure you are finished, check that you have done every example.* It's frustrating to lose points because you skipped a question by mistake.

10. *Save the last few minutes to reread your answers to make sure they are correct and complete.* Don't change any answers unless you have at least one good reason for doing so.

Follow-up

1. *Learn from your mistakes.* Go over your corrected test carefully. Notice where you did especially well. What mistakes did you make? Figure out why you made them. Did you have problems with the material? Or just misunderstand some part of the question? Next time around, spend extra time on the problems that tripped you up. Either study more or take extra care on the test itself.

2. *Save your corrected test.* Use your corrected tests as study tools for finals. Take special note of your strengths and weaknesses, so you will know how to study for the next test.

3. *Go out and celebrate.* If you followed a lot of this advice, you probably did very well on your most recent test. Now that it's over, treat yourself to something you postponed while you were studying. You deserve it!

5
What's on Your Mind? Some Answers to Students' Questions

What are kids really worried about when it comes to school? What questions would they most like to have answered in a book like this one? A large group of middle-schoolers like you were asked to come up with questions. To their questions, others have been added that have been asked for years. This chapter includes questions and answers — grouped by topic — from real students.

Here is what was on the minds of these students. Maybe you will find some answers to your own problems as you read through.

Problems on the Home Front

Decisions

QUESTION: *My problem is I can't make decisions, even about small things. Some days I can't even decide what to wear or what to have for lunch. Lots of times I can't make up my mind about which homework to do first. Then, by the time I decide, it's too late. Help!*

ANSWER: Making good decisions takes practice. Your family may have been making a lot of decisions for you so far, so you haven't practiced enough on your own yet.

Here are some tips for helping decide about the problems you mention:

• Deciding what to wear. Listen to the weather forecast each night. Think about whether you have gym or some other special activity the next day. Based on the weather and your plans for the next day, choose the outfit that you like best. Stick with your decision in the morning no matter what.

• Deciding what to have for lunch. Do you bring your own lunch, and you can't decide what to make? List your four favorite lunches. Have your parents stock one favorite per week for four weeks, then start the cycle again. Do you buy lunch at school? Schools usually publish menus a week ahead. Go over the menus at home where things are less chaotic. Pick out the favorite meal for each day of the week and stick with it.

• Deciding what homework to do first. Do the most difficult homework first to get it out of the way.

Whenever you have to make a decision, give yourself a few minutes to think of the pros and cons. Then go with one choice and stay with it, knowing you have already worked out all your reasons.

Room-Sharing and Noise

QUESTION: *I have to share my room with my older sister. Even though I have my own desk and bookcase and try to keep things organized, my sister messes up the room. Plus, just when I want to study, she wants to play her tape recorder. All we do is fight. Sometimes I wish I were an only child. How am I supposed to get my work done in the middle of all this?*

ANSWER: Sharing a room is hard. Try talking to your sister when you are both calm and not fighting. See if you and your sister can decide on a time when you can each count on having the room alone. If that isn't practical, try to work out a daily quiet period when no talking, music, phone calls, or friends are allowed in the bedroom. Remember, the deal has to work both ways; you each have to contribute equally to the plan. If your sister is still uncooperative and your parents aren't any help either, here are some plans to work out on your own. Do your homework during free periods at school. Or work when you know your sister is out of the house or watching her favorite TV show downstairs. Find a quiet study spot elsewhere in your house. Get earplugs. Use that bookcase to divide your side of the room from hers, so that you don't have to look at each other as often. Hope she gets a boyfriend who calls her every night for two hours on the hall phone!

Bad Report Card

QUESTION: *I'm not the greatest student, and the last time I came home with a bad report card, my parents went crazy. They screamed and yelled, cut off my allowance, and grounded me for a month. I'm trying to do better at school, but I'm scared of what will happen if I get bad grades again. I feel like running away from home.*

ANSWER: Don't run away! First, read this book and follow some of the suggestions in it to improve your grades. It may take a little time before your grades improve. Meanwhile, here's what to do about a bad report card you know is coming. If there are still a few weeks left, go see your teachers and ask if there is any extra work you can do to pull up your grades now. Occasionally, teachers allow students to retake a test, write an extra paper, or make up missing homework. Then talk to your parents *right away*. Tell them you think you might

54

be getting a bad grade, and you have already started doing something about it. They won't be as likely to ground you or withhold privileges if you tell them how you plan to set aside extra time every day for studying. Most parents respond well to signs of independence and determination like this from their kids. Maybe you have parents like that. In any case, prepare your family ahead of time for possible bad news. Then give them the good news about *your* study plans ahead of time. Doing this may prevent a big blowup at report card time. Good luck.

Interfering Parents

QUESTION: *I turn in some of the best homework and reports in my class. Know why? Because my parents do a lot of it for me. It's not as much fun as you might think either. If I get a good grade, I don't feel that great about it because it's not really mine. And sometimes I get a bad grade on work I do in class because I'm so used to having my parents do it better. How can I get them to stop interfering with school?*

ANSWER: This is a common problem and hard to cure. Parents are sometimes too eager to share their own knowledge. Or sometimes this bad habit begins when a parent starts out by supervising the homework, then correcting or redoing the mistakes themselves. Before they know it, they have changed the work so much, it doesn't really belong to their child anymore. The homework is yours; the grades are yours. Tell your parents it's okay for them to check your work, but that you want to be responsible for doing it. Let them know that you will learn the material better if you do the actual work yourself.

Problems at School

I'm Late

QUESTION: *No matter what I do, I'm always late for everything. Now that I have so many classes, the problem is even worse.*

ANSWER: Here are some things to help you get to where you're going on time:

• Be a clock-watcher. Give yourself mini deadlines to complete certain jobs — for example, ten minutes to shower; fifteen minutes to get dressed; twenty minutes for breakfast. You may find yourself running on time or even a little ahead.

• Some other tips: Set your own deadlines rather than depending on other people to make you on time. Try to follow the same routine every day. Get up at the same time; put your clothes and books in the same place; finish breakfast by a certain time, and so on. At school, give yourself a little deadline for getting to each class. You'll be amazed at how breaking up your long school day into shorter parts will help you become more punctual.

Too Many Subjects and Teachers

QUESTION: *Sometimes I wish I could go back to a lower grade. I only had one main teacher then, and she didn't give us as much homework. I have so many teachers now, it took me three weeks to learn their names. Sometimes they all pile up the homework on the same night or give tests on the same day. I can't keep it all straight in my head. How can I straighten out one class from another?*

ANSWER: This is one of the toughest problems middle-schoolers have to cope with. It's hard to see new faces and deal with new personalities every forty minutes or so. And it's even harder to keep track of so much different work. It is quite true that teachers aren't always aware of conflicts. If you feel comfortable with your teacher, let her know that the math teacher has a big test planned the same day as your science test. If that's too hard to do, then check your calendar for upcoming tests and projects. Try to figure out *separate* study schedules for each test or project. Set aside the most time for the hardest subject. Another possibility is to study with one or two other people in class. Break down the big study job into smaller ones. One of you can get the class notes up-to-date. Another person can make up possible test questions. One person can do the heavy-duty reading and take notes for the rest of you. Sharing jobs like this will give you each more time to study for any conflicting tests.

Asking for Help

QUESTION: *All my teachers ever seem to do is pile on the work or lecture me about stuff I forgot to do. Sometimes they can be nice, but most of the time, I'm afraid of my teachers. If only they could read my mind. Are teachers for real?*

ANSWER: Believe it or not, most teachers are real. And the best way to find out if they are real is to talk to them one to one. This isn't always easy since teachers and students in middle school have such busy schedules. What a lot of students don't realize is that there are ways of talking over problems with teachers *before* they get to a crisis.

Here are a few ways to get a teacher on your side if you are having difficulties in a class:

• If you miss an assignment, or you know you did a poor job, go to class a little early and tell the teacher right away. Most teachers only find these things out when they are correcting papers at home, and you are not there to defend yourself. Tell your teacher — honestly — why you are missing a paper or couldn't do a good job. Ask for help, or offer a plan for redoing or making up the work. Most teachers will be very impressed by a student who goes halfway like this.

• If you are doing poorly in a class, don't wait until the report card comes out to see your teacher. Every time you get a low grade on a test or paper, see your teacher after class to find out how you can improve *next* time. Teachers are there to help you, but they can't help if they don't know what the problem is. Let them know what it is you don't understand. But don't wait until the last minute when it is too late.

• Get yourself in a good bargaining position if you want your teachers to give you an extra chance or some special help. Even if an assignment is really hard, *do some of it* to show your good intentions. Be on time. Behave in class. Have your materials with you all the time. Answer questions in class once in a while. Look alive. Even if you can't figure out long division, it doesn't take any special skills in math to show up promptly, to listen carefully, and to ignore the kids who are hacking around and steaming up the teacher. Decent behavior doesn't cost anything but does pay off, even when you don't understand the subject very well. If you score points on attitude, your teacher is much more likely to be on your side if you ask for special attention or second chances.

Older Kids Who Tease

QUESTION: *Sometimes I hate going to school. I like my teachers and my friends, but lots of times the older kids bug me in the hallways or in the playground. It makes me feel like crying, and my face always gets red. How can I get rid of these kids?*

ANSWER: The surest way to get rid of these older kids who bug you is to make them disappear. How? Imagine that they are totally invisible. Do not answer them when they speak. Treat them as if they are simply not there. However, if someone gets physical — pushes, shoves, or grabs your property, tell the person to stop. If this doesn't work and things get out of hand, get the courage together to go to the teacher or the principal's office and report that person. No one has the right to shove you around or take your property. This advice will be hard to follow because it takes time for these peanut-butter brains to get the message.

But stick with it. After a while when they see they can't get a reaction out of you (or they get themselves into trouble by going too far), they will lay off. And remember, you won't be this age forever. Someday you will be an older kid, too.

Problem Friends

QUESTION: *I do okay in school, but my best friends goof off. I want them to stay friends with me, but they tease me about being teacher's pet just because I get good grades. What can I do?*

ANSWER: Try to enjoy your friends as much as you can out of school and during free periods. Maybe some of them are having problems in school. You could invite them over to study together. If your friends still bug you about school, get friendly with a couple of other kids who are more like you. After a while you won't have to depend on your old friends as much. Good luck!

Homework and Tests

Putting Things Off

QUESTION: *I know I'm supposed to do my work a little bit at a time, but I always wind up doing it at the last minute. Then it's a mess. Why do I keep doing this? How can I stop?*

ANSWER: Everybody puts off jobs they don't want to do once in a while. It's a bad habit, though, if it means you wind up doing a poor job. People who put things off usually have unrealistic goals about how a project is going to turn out. In their minds, their paper is going to be the best one in the class. Or they are going to get a hundred on the test. As long as they postpone working or studying, they can still fantasize about how great they are going to do. Working on the dull details of a project ruins the fantasy. Does this kind of thinking sound familiar? If it does, that may be why you put things off. Now it's time to tell yourself that you may not get an A+ or 100, but that you will do the *best* job possible. And the best job possible isn't something you can do at the last minute. As soon as you have a test or project deadline, promise yourself to do *something* on it every night — no matter how small. Five minutes is better than no minutes. One line is better than a blank sheet of paper. Just doing one thing will at least get your mind in motion and some ideas going. So, if you do wind up doing most of the work at the last minute, you won't be starting totally from scratch. It's going to take a while before you get over the postponing habit, but keep working on it.

Cramming

QUESTION: *Why do I always start cramming the night before?*

ANSWER: Crammers like to tell themselves that if only they had had the time, they would have gotten 100 instead of 72 on a test. Or an A+ instead of a C−. The people who cram are usually the same ones who put things off. Read over some of the suggestions in the preceding answer to see if that description fits you. Cramming is the surest way to ruin your appetite, your sleep, and your peace of mind. So cut it out. Do a little bit each day, even if it's just writing your name on the sheet or completing one example. Now that that's settled, here's some advice on how to cram if you have gotten yourself into this situation. Cramming is excusable if you are just getting over the chicken pox, just got back from a trip, or went to sleep for two weeks and woke up the night before a big exam.

Here's what to do:

• Find a place to study with no distractions. Give

yourself at least one hour to study.

• Skim all your class notes and handout sheets.

• Skim over the sections of your textbook that you were supposed to study for the test.

• Write down a word or two about important ideas as you read.

• You won't have time to memorize. Instead, read terms and definitions out loud a few times each.

• If you are taking a math test, quickly work out two or three examples from the book.

• Go to bed at your normal time and get up at your normal time. Losing sleep is only going to make that jumble of information worse.

• Get to class early. Do a lot of deep breathing to calm your nerves.

• After you take the test, promise yourself you will never cram again — ever!

Cheating

QUESTION: *One of my friends gets good grades by cheating on some of the tests we have to take. Her parents are really strict about school, so she's afraid of getting bad grades. Once or twice she asked me to cheat, too, when we sat next to each other. I said no, but it sure makes me mad when she gets a better grade than I do. Tell me what to do.*

ANSWER: Keep saying no to the cheating. Sooner or later, she is going to get caught, and you won't want to be any part of that. Your friend probably feels awful about her cheating. She may want you to join her to make the cheating more acceptable to herself. Maybe your friend doesn't really know how to prepare for a test on her own. You might suggest studying together as an alternative.

Studying with a Friend

QUESTION: *My best friend and I try to study for tests together, but we always wind up talking, laughing, or eating instead. I think we sometimes do worse on tests than if we studied alone. I thought studying with another person was supposed to help you out on tests. Should we keep studying together?*

ANSWER: Try studying together only if you can really do the following:

• On your own (and on her own), catch up on all your old notes and read over the material that will be covered on the test. Do this a day or two *before* you get together with your friend.

• Do all your memorizing *before* the two of you get together.

• Before you get together, each write down a couple of questions you think the teacher might ask.

• Do not get together unless you promise each other to spend at least half an hour studying for the test. Set aside this half hour *at the beginning* of the visit.

• Spend fifteen minutes reading over each other's class notes, old homework, and tests.

• Spend the last fifteen minutes quizzing each other with the questions you each made up.

• After the half hour is over, go to the kitchen. Get a snack. Spend at least a half hour talking, laughing, and eating. You deserve it!

Nervous About Tests:

QUESTION: *Even though I study for tests, I'm a nervous wreck when I have to take a test. My heart starts pounding. I drop my pencil. I forget what I studied. How can I calm down?*

ANSWER: A little nervousness is a good thing. It gets your mind in gear and gives you a spurt of energy. It does sound as if your nervousness is causing problems, though. First, think about what's making you nervous. Are you worried about getting a bad grade? Are you afraid if you don't do well, your parents will get mad? Do you think you have to get a great grade every time? Keep in mind that test scores are only one part of your final grade. Your homework, papers, class participation, and behavior count for just as much — more — than just one test.

Now that you know that, here are some other tips to get yourself calmed down:

• Follow the study tips in Chapter 4 of this book. If you do, you will have a good solid foundation for the test.

• Do make sure you study a little bit at a time. Avoid cramming the night before or the morning of the test.

• Go to sleep and get up at the regular time on test day so you'll feel rested.

• Get to class a little early, but don't use those few extra minutes to study. Instead, close your eyes or daydream about something soothing — waves lapping on a shore; someone rubbing your forehead. Or slowly doodle on a piece of paper. Clench your fists, then very slowly unclench them. Do all this before the teacher starts talking or hands out the test. If you find yourself getting tense during the test, try one of these exercises again to relax yourself.

• Have a plan for doing the test. Do the easiest examples first to build your self-confidence. (If some sections are worth more than others, do the easiest of the most valuable questions first.)

• Don't get stuck on a question; that will just

make you more nervous. Move right on to something you can answer. You can always go back later.

• Remember, it's only a test. The rest of your work counts for a lot, too. And there will be other tests.

6
Quick Review:
A School Survival Kit

What do you do when you need to get in shape for school fast? When you want to change those C's to B's or A's? When you are determined to catch up on your homework once and for all? Or when you just want to get off to a good start as the new semester begins? This School Survival Kit lists a few shortcuts to get yourself on track quickly. Check it out whenever you need help in a hurry.

School Tools: A Checklist

Can't Live Without
- [x] Three-ring notebook with subject dividers.
- [x] Assignment pad.
- [ ] Extra class schedules (home, notebook, locker).
- [x] Extra supplies — three-ring notebook paper, extra pens and pencils — half at home, half in your locker.
- [x] Phone number of a student in each class.
- [x] Library card.
- [ ] Dictionary.
- [x] Book bag or backpack.

Great To Have
- [ ] Bulletin board at home.
- [x] Large wall calendar for appointments and deadlines.
- [x] Wristwatch and alarm clock.
- [ ] Cassette tape recorder.
- [ ] Thesaurus.
- [x] Earplugs.

A Listening-Skills Checklist

- ☑ Do all your work before going to class.
- ☑ Be on time.
- ☑ Open your notebook when you sit down.
- ☑ Make eye contact with the teacher.
- ☑ Stay involved by asking or answering questions.
- ☑ Take notes.

A Note-Taking-Skills Checklist

- ☑ Write the date on each set of notes and handout sheets.
- ☑ Underline important words in your notes and on handouts.
- ☑ Save all handout sheets in the proper section of your notebook.
- ☑ When the teacher says, "Write it down," write it down.
- ☑ Copy what the teacher puts on the blackboard.
- ☑ If you miss a class, borrow someone else's notes or get the handout sheets from the teacher when you return.
- ☑ Read each day's notes when you do your homework.
- ☑ Reread all notes and handouts covered on a test.

71

A Homework-Skills Checklist

In Class

☑ Write down each assignment and due date.

☑ Ask questions when you don't understand the homework.

☑ Know what books and materials you have to take home that day.

At Home

☑ Write down long-term assignments, test days, etc., on a big wall calendar.

☑ Check your calendar every day.

☑ Figure out the best time of day to do homework.

☑ Work on the hardest homework first.

☑ Complete all the homework you can.

If you get stuck, try this:

☑ • Reread your class notes, handouts, or book to see if the answer is in one of those places.

☑ • Move on to other homework, then go back to the hard part.

☑ • Call a classmate or ask a family member for help.

At Home

☑ • If you still can't complete the work, write a note to your teacher and clip it to the homework you did finish. Ask your teacher for help *before* you hand in the assignment.

☑ Reread each assignment as you finish it.

☑ Check your assignment pad one more time to make sure you have done everything.

☑ Put your homework and books in your book-bag.

☑ If you made mistakes on your homework, find out why when you get it back, so you don't repeat the mistakes again.

☑ Save all homework to study from at test time.

A Memorizing Checklist

☑ Do your memorizing at the beginning of your study time.

☑ Make sure you understand the material before you try to memorize it.

☑ Write down what you want to memorize. *Or:* Repeat out loud what you want to memorize until you can recite it back automatically. *Or:* If you have a tape recorder, use it to help in memorizing.

☑ Read what you want to memorize into a tape recorder and keep playing it back. *Or:* Quiz yourself on tape.

☑ Keep rereading what you want to memorize until you can "see" it in your mind.

☑ Have a family member quiz you on what you've memorized.

A Test-Taking Checklist

Studying for a Test

☑ Find out what material is going to be covered on the test.

☑ Copy the test date onto a big calendar.

☑ Plan a study schedule so that you do a little each day. Set aside a longer amount of time on the two nights before.

☑ Catch up on missing assignments and notes right away.

☑ Do your memorizing a little bit at a time every day.

☑ Skim your class notes and handout sheets.

☑ Skim old tests and homework assignments.

☑ Skim your textbook chapters.

☑ Answer questions at the end of chapters in your head.

☑ Ask for help on any material you don't understand.

☑ Think of a few questions the teacher might ask and answer them in your head.

☑ Quiz yourself the night before, or study with a friend and quiz each other.

☑ Go to bed on time. Have a good breakfast on test day. Bring what you will need to school.

Taking the Test

- ☑ Arrive a little early with all your materials — extra paper, two pens, two pencils, and an eraser.
- ☑ Listen carefully to the teacher's directions.
- ☑ Write your name and the date on the test sheet.
- ☑ Read carefully any written directions, under-lining important words as you read.
- ☑ Figure out a quick schedule of how much time to spend on each question. Devote more time to questions that are worth the most.
- ☑ Leave a few minutes at the end for rereading the test.
- ☐ Work on the easiest examples first. (However, if some sections are worth more than others, do the easiest of the most valuable questions first.)
- ☑ Go back to the harder questions. Guess answers if you have to.
- ☑ When you have finished, check that you did each question.
- ☑ Reread the test to make sure you haven't made any mistakes.
- ☐ Check that your paper is neat and easy to read. Don't change any answers unless you have at least one good reason for doing so.

Taking the Test

☑ Save all your tests to learn from your mistakes. Old tests make good study sheets for final exams.

Tip-off

Ten Top Tips from Students Who Made It Through Middle School

• *"Don't wait till the last minute; start studying early."*

• *"Write everything, but* everything, *down. It's the only way you'll remember what you're supposed to."*

• *"Reread everything you do."*

• *"Don't throw out anything your teacher hands out."*

• *"Don't worry; just do it."*

• *"Take notes and keep them where you can find them. Dittos, too."*

• *"Be on time no matter what."*

• *"Keep everything in one notebook."*

• *"Don't worry if you don't make friends the first day."*

• *"It gets easier, so hang in there."*

Go for the Goal:
Habits To Work on in the Future

_____

_____

_____

_____

_____

_____

_____

_____

_____

_____

_____

_____

_____

_____

_____

_____

_____

_____

_____

_____

_____

_____

Go for the Goal:
Habits To Work on in the Future

_____

_____

_____

_____

_____

_____

_____

_____

_____

_____

_____

_____

_____

_____

_____

_____

_____

_____

_____

_____

_____

_____

_____

_____

Test Record Sheet

Course	Type of Test	Date
EVarmol setes	maps	Dec 3

Grade	Strong and Weak Points
4	Strong Points

Test Record Sheet

Course	Type of Test	Date

Grade	Strong and Weak Points

Student's Notes

Student's Notes

Student's Notes

INDEX